C. 1

Symbols of
American Freedom

Independence
Hall

by Hilarie Staton

Series Consultant: Jerry D. Thompson,
Regents Professor of History,
Texas A&M International University

**CHELSEA
CLUBHOUSE**
An Imprint of Chelsea House Publishers

Symbols of American Freedom: Independence Hall

Chelsea Clubhouse
An imprint of Chelsea House Publishers
132 West 31st Street
New York NY 10001

Library of Congress Cataloging-in-Publication Data
Staton, Hilarie.
    Independence Hall / by Hilarie Staton.
        p. cm. — (Symbols of American freedom)
    Includes index.
    ISBN 978-1-60413-521-3
    1. Independence Hall (Philadelphia, Pa.—Juvenile literature. 2. United States—Politics and government—1775-1783—Juvenile literature. 3. United States—Politics and government—1783-1789—Juvenile literature. 4. Philadelphia (Pa.)—Buildings, structures, etc.—Juvenile literature. I. Title. II. Series.
    F158.8.I3S73 2010
    974.8'11—dc22   2009012824

Chelsea Clubhouse books are available at special discounts when purchased in bulk quantities for businesses, associations, institutions, or sales promotions. Please call our Special Sales Department in New York at (212) 967-8800 or (800) 322-8755.

You can find Chelsea Clubhouse on the World Wide Web at http://www.chelseahouse.com

Developed for Chelsea House by RJF Publishing LLC (www.RJFpublishing.com)
Text and cover design by Tammy West/Westgraphix LLC
Maps by Stefan Chabluk
Photo research by Edward A. Thomas
Index by Nila Glikin

Photo Credits: 5: Library of Congress LC-USZ62-9486; 7: Indianapolis Museum of Art/The Bridgeman Art Library; 8: age fotostock/Photolibrary; 9: © Edward A. Thomas; 13: Library of Congress LC-USZC4-12538; 15: Look and Learn/The Bridgeman Art Library; 16: Library of Congress LC-USZC4-7214; 19: Library of Congress LC-USZC4-9904; 21: Library of Congress LC-USZC4-6877; 23: Library of Congress LC-USZCN4-220; 24: Library of Congress LC-DIG-hec-03838; 25: © SuperStock, Inc./SuperStock; 26: © Joseph Sohm/Visions of America/Corbis; 29: Library of Congress LC-USZ62-70508; 31: Library of Congress LC-USZ62-2357; 33: North Wind Photo Archives/Photolibrary; 34: North Wind Photo Archives/Photolibrary; 36: Library of Congress LC-DIG-det-4a28035; 37: Library of Congress LC-DIG-hec-06745; 41: Library of Congress LC-USZC4-9905; 42: Corbis/Photolibrary; 43: iStockphoto.

Printed and bound in the United States of America

Bang RJF 10 9 8 7 6 5 4 3 2 1

This book is printed on acid-free paper.

All links and Web addresses were checked and verified to be correct at the time of publication. Because of the dynamic nature of the Web, some addresses and links may have changed since publication and may no longer be valid.

Note: Quotations in the text are used essentially as originally written. In some cases, spelling, punctuation, and the like have been modernized to aid student understanding.

Table of Contents

Words that are defined in the Glossary are in **bold** type the first time they appear in the text.

Independence Hall: More Than a Place

The building where the United States was born still stands in Philadelphia, Pennsylvania. In this building, then called the Pennsylvania State House, two important documents were **adopted** in the late 1700s: the Declaration of **Independence** and the U.S. **Constitution**. These documents are about independence and freedom, so people later called the building Independence Hall. It became a **symbol** of, or stood for, freedom. The bell that hung in its tower was called the Liberty Bell. It also became a popular symbol of freedom.

A Building Where History Was Made

Pennsylvania in the 1700s was one of the thirteen British **colonies** that would form the United States. Philadelphia was an important city in the British colonies. The Pennsylvania State House was the largest building in Philadelphia and one of the most beautiful in all the colonies. Pennsylvania's **Assembly**, a group of men elected to help the governor run the colony, met there.

By 1774, many colonists did not like the way the British government was treating its colonies. One problem was taxes. The American colonies had to pay taxes to the British government. But the colonies did not have any **representatives** in the British Parliament, the group of men in London (Great Britain's **capital** city) that passed laws about taxes and other matters. Twelve of the colonies sent **delegates** to the First Continental Congress, which met at a building called Carpenters' Hall in Philadelphia to discuss what to do. The delegates sent a list of their complaints to the British king, but things only got worse.

This picture shows Independence Hall as it looked in the late 1700s. Then called the Pennsylvania State House, it was the largest building in Philadelphia.

The thirteen colonies (shown in blue) won their independence in the American Revolution. They also gained new land after the war.

Delegates from all thirteen colonies met again in Philadelphia beginning in 1775. This time the delegates met in the State House. They met in a large room called the Assembly Room, where the Pennsylvania Assembly held its meetings.

By the time this Second Continental Congress began, fighting had already started between colonists and British soldiers. In 1776, the delegates decided that the colonies should break away from Great Britain and become an independent country. Thomas Jefferson wrote the Declaration of Independence, giving the reasons why the colonies were separating from

Great Britain. The delegates discussed the Declaration in the Assembly Room, and in that room they voted to approve it on July 4, 1776. It was read to people for the first time outside the State House a few days later. After it was sent to the British king, the Continental Congress continued to meet at the State House.

The colonies fought a long war with Great Britain to win their freedom. George Washington was picked by the Continental Congress to lead the colonists' Continental Army during the war. At the end of this American Revolution (1775–1783), the new country had won its independence. The United States of America had been born. The former thirteen colonies were now thirteen states within the United States.

George Washington is shown here in the uniform he wore as leader of the Continental Army.

Facts About the Liberty Bell

- Made in 1752 at Whitechapel Foundry in England

- Melted down and remade twice by Pass and Stow in Philadelphia

- Made of 70% copper and 25% tin, with small amounts of other metals and of arsenic

- Crack: ½ inch (1.3 centimeters) wide and 24½ inches (62 centimeters) long; there are also several small cracks

- 12 feet ½ inch (3.7 meters) around its bottom lip

- 6 feet 11¼ inches (2.1 meters) around its top (crown)

- Total height: 5 feet 3 inches (1.6 meters)

- Thickness of metal at lip: 3 inches (7.6 centimeters)

- Thickness of metal at crown 1¼ inches (3.2 centimeters)

- Weight: 2,080 pounds (943 kilograms)

- Length of **clapper**: 3 feet 2 inches (1 meter)

- Weight of clapper: 44½ pounds (20 kilograms)

The Liberty Bell can still be seen in Philadelphia. It is now on display in its own building near Independence Hall.

New Government for a New Country

By 1786, many people were not happy with the way the new country's government was working. The next year, delegates met at the State House and decided to write a constitution, or new plan of government. They talked and argued and finally agreed on a new U.S. Constitution. Then, the states ratified, or approved, it. The men who agreed on the Declaration of Independence and wrote the Constitution are often called the Founding Fathers. At the State House they founded, or created, the United States and created the nation's government.

George Washington was sworn in as the first president of the United States at Federal Hall in New York City in 1789. Then, in 1790, the government moved from New York to Philadelphia, which remained the capital for ten years. By 1800, both the U.S. government and Pennsylvania's state government had moved to other cities, but Philadelphia's city government continued to use the State House building.

Remembering the Past

In 1824, the Marquis de Lafayette visited the State House. Lafayette was a Frenchman who had fought with the Continental Army and became a hero of the American Revolution. He reminded people of what happened in the State House building. People began calling it Independence Hall. It became a symbol of the liberty that was promised to Americans in the Declaration of Independence and the Constitution.

As the city of Philadelphia grew, tall buildings towered over Independence Hall, but people never completely forgot it. The city, state, and national governments worked to restore it and other nearby historic buildings, to create a park, and to tell the story of American independence.

The Liberty Bell and Independence Square

In 1751, the Assembly had ordered a new bell to hang in the State House bell tower. Originally made in England (part of Great Britain), the bell cracked

Each year, millions of people visit Independence Hall and other historic buildings in the center of the modern city of Philadelphia.

the first time it was rung, and a Philadelphia company had to remake it twice to fix the problem. After that, it was rung many times. In the 1830s, people working to end slavery in the United States began calling it the Liberty Bell. It became a symbol to people fighting for freedom. In the 1840s, the bell cracked again, and that crack is still there. Today, the Liberty Bell remains a symbol of freedom. Many people go to see it in Philadelphia, and many more people have seen pictures of the bell and its now-famous crack.

Originally, the State House bell was rung to call the Assembly to a meeting or to tell everyone there was important news. Crowds gathered in the open area, called the State House Yard, in front of the building to hear that news and to discuss what it meant. Later, the yard was renamed Independence Square, and it continued to be an important place for celebrations and **demonstrations**. People celebrated the country's independence there every Fourth of July. At other times, they demonstrated to show that they were unhappy with how they or other people were being treated. Presidents and vice presidents gave speeches to huge crowds there.

Visiting the Symbols Today

Today, Independence Hall is in the center of a big city. Three square blocks of the city have been made into Independence National Historical Park. This area includes Independence Hall, a building where the Liberty Bell can be seen, and other nearby buildings. More than 3 million people visit the park each year.

How Many Visitors

Independence Hall is one of the most visited sites related to the birth of the United States. About 3 million people a year visit Yorktown, Virginia, where the Continental Army won the last major battle of the Revolution. About 1 million people a year visit George Washington's Virginia home, Mount Vernon.

Chapter 2

Birthplace of the United States

In 1681, Englishman William Penn was given land in America by Charles II, king of Great Britain, and allowed to start a new colony. Penn was a **Quaker**, and people who practiced this religion were not treated well in England. The new colony was named Pennsylvania, which means "Penn's woods." Penn made sure his colony allowed religious freedom. Not only Quakers but all people in Pennsylvania could practice whatever religion they wanted. The Pennsylvania Assembly was an elected group of colonists that helped Penn (and later other governors) run the colony. In 1701, Penn and the Assembly wrote the Charter of Privileges. It described the colonial government and protected individual rights, including religious freedom.

Philadelphia, which means "city of brotherly love" in Greek, was the capital of the Pennsylvania colony. It was an important center of trade, politics, and learning. Many

Colonial Philadelphia

Philadelphia grew from only 5,000 people in the 1720s to about 40,000 by the 1770s. At the time that the Declaration of Independence was written, Philadelphia had more people than any other city in the thirteen colonies. Many trading ships left Philadelphia and went to the West Indies with flour and lumber. (The West Indies are a chain of islands south of the eastern United States in the Caribbean Sea.) The ships returned with rum, sugar, molasses, and hard wood that was used to make furniture and other things. Ships from England brought goods to sell.

A view of the city of Philadelphia in 1768.

people moved to the city and began businesses there. One of them was Benjamin Franklin, who became one of Philadelphia's most important leaders and one of the Founding Fathers.

Building a State House

Andrew Hamilton was a leader in the Pennsylvania Assembly, and he wanted the Assembly to have its own meeting place. He worked with master carpenter Edmund Woolley to design the State House. They began building it in 1732, but it was not completely finished for 21 years. The Assembly began meeting in its Assembly Room in 1742.

A new **steeple** was added to the building in 1753. Two years earlier, the Assembly had ordered a bell from England to celebrate the 50th anniversary of Penn's Charter of Privileges. They asked that the bell have on it a line from the Bible. They thought this line symbolized the freedoms given to them in the Charter. It said, "Proclaim Liberty throughout all the land unto all the inhabitants thereof."

The bell cracked the first time it rang. Two Philadelphia metal workers, John Pass and John Stow, were asked to melt the bell and use the metal to make a new one. But people did not like the sound of this new bell, so Pass and Stow tried again. This one did not sound right either, so a new bell was ordered from England. When it came, people said it did not sound much better. The first bell was hung in the State House steeple, and the newer one was attached to a clock that rang the time.

Hamilton's State House was a beautiful two-story brick building, the largest in the city. It had a central hall with a large room on each side, one for the Assembly and one for the Pennsylvania Supreme Court.

The Path to Independence

By the 1750s, each colony had its own government, but many laws still came from Great Britain. In the 1760s, the British Parliament passed new taxes that the colonists had to pay and new controls on the colonies' trade. Most colonists did not like these changes. They were angry that laws about taxes had been passed without giving the colonists a say. The colonists called this taxation without **representation**. Some colonists joined together to let the British government know what they thought. As a result, Great Britain ended some taxes and some limits on the colonies' trade. A tax on tea brought into the colonies was continued.

Then, in 1773, the colonists learned that the British government was letting only one company, the British East India Company, sell tea in the colonies. Many people became angry about this and about the continuing tax on tea. In the city of Boston, a group of colonists (dressed as Native Americans) boarded ships loaded with tea and dumped the tea into Boston Harbor. This event became known as the Boston Tea Party. In Pennsylvania, the Assembly said that it would not allow ships to unload tea. The tea had to be taken back to England.

The British government took action to punish the colonies and especially the city of Boston. On June 1, 1774, the British closed Boston Harbor, upsetting many colonists. Then, on June 18, thousands of colonists met in Philadelphia in the State House Yard. The people at the meeting agreed to share ideas with the other colonies. All the colonies except Georgia decided to send delegates to a meeting in Philadelphia to discuss what to do. The meeting was supposed to take place in the State House. But before the delegates arrived, Pennsylvania's governor called the Assembly into a special meeting. He did not want Pennsylvania delegates to support any action against Britain. Because of that, the First Continental Congress refused to meet in the State House. Instead it met in a new building called Carpenters' Hall.

This painting, done much later, shows colonists throwing British tea into the harbor at the Boston Tea Party.

Benjamin Franklin (1706–1790)

Benjamin Franklin was one of the most successful businessmen in the American colonies. He was also a great writer and inventor. As a leader in Philadelphia, he improved the city in many ways. And during and after the American Revolution, he was one of the most important Founding Fathers of the new nation.

Franklin was born in Boston in 1706. When he was twelve, he started working for his older brother, who was a printer. But his brother would beat him, so when he was seventeen, Franklin ran away. He arrived in Philadelphia in 1723 and quickly found a job with a printer. He soon made his first trip to England and stayed to learn more about printing. He returned to Philadelphia and became involved in many things. He published a newspaper that became very successful, and every year for twenty-five years he published *Poor Richard's Almanack*, a book of facts and clever sayings. He also did experiments with electricity, among other things. He invented many things to make life better, including a stove (which became known as the Franklin stove) that heated rooms much better than a fireplace. He began the first library in Philadelphia, the city's first fire company, the city's first public hospital, and a college that became the University of Pennsylvania.

Franklin was in England during the First Continental Congress, but he played an important part at the Second Continental Congress. He supported independence, even though his son was the governor of New Jersey and supported the British. During the American Revolution, Franklin went to France and played an important part in getting the French government to help the colonists fight the British. After returning to Philadelphia, he attended the Constitutional **Convention** that wrote the U.S. Constitution. In 1790, a year after George Washington became president, Franklin died at the age of 84.

The First Continental Congress met from September 5 to October 26, 1774. The delegates sent King George III of Great Britain a list of their complaints. They planned to meet again in May 1775 if things had not improved.

Six months later, the State House bell rang to call people to a meeting at the State House Yard. There, people heard about the battles between colonists and British troops on April 19, 1775, at Lexington and Concord in Massachusetts. More and more colonists decided they did not want to continue living under British rule. In Philadelphia, some people began to practice marching and shooting in case they had to protect the city.

"Free and Independent States"

The Second Continental Congress began meeting in Philadelphia on May 10, 1775. One of the first things the delegates did was to create the Continental Army to protect the colonies. They voted to make George Washington the commander-in-chief of that army and sent him to Boston to fight the British.

Congress had not heard from King George III about their complaints, so they spent the next year discussing their choices. Some wanted the colonies to become an independent country. Others wanted to work with the British government and remain under British rule. Then, they learned that the king did not agree with anything they said. After that, more colonists supported breaking away from Britain.

On June 7, 1776, Richard Henry Lee, one of the delegates from Virginia, asked Congress to form an independent country. Declaring independence was a very important step, so the delegates agreed to wait for three weeks before they made their final decision. They appointed a **committee** of five delegates to write a statement that would tell the king why they wanted independence.

Thomas Jefferson (1743–1826)

Thomas Jefferson was one of the youngest delegates at the Second Continental Congress. He was born in Virginia in 1743, and he went to college and studied law in Williamsburg, the capital of the colony. He owned a **plantation** in Virginia and also practiced law. During the American Revolution, Jefferson was a leader in the government of Virginia. After the war, he was the new country's minister (ambassador) to France, and he was in France when the Constitutional Convention met. When George Washington was president, Jefferson was the secretary of state. He was vice president under John Adams, the second president of the United States. Jefferson was elected the third president and served from 1801 to 1809. As president, he greatly expanded the size of the United States when he purchased the Louisiana Territory from France in 1803. Jefferson read many books. In 1814, after the original Library of Congress was burned during the War of 1812 (1812–1815), Jefferson gave the government his huge collection of books to start a new library. Jefferson died on the fiftieth anniversary of the Declaration of Independence, July 4, 1826, just hours before John Adams died.

Thomas Jefferson, Benjamin Franklin, John Adams, Roger Sherman, and Robert R. Livingston were the members of the committee. They decided that, since Jefferson was the best writer, he should write the statement. He worked for two weeks in his room. He thought carefully about what to say and how to say it. He wanted to convince people everywhere that fighting for independence was the right thing to do. He asked Franklin and Adams to read what he had written. They made a few changes, but not many.

On July 2, 1776, the delegates at the Continental Congress voted in favor of the colonies' becoming independent from Great Britain. Then they discussed Jefferson's Declaration of Independence. In it was a list of their complaints and the ideas they believed in. It said that all men are created equal and that people in the colonies were not being treated as equals by Great Britain. This gave them the right to create a new country.

On July 4, 1776, the Continental Congress approved the Declaration of Independence. That day, the State House became the birthplace of the United States of America.

In Their Own Words

From the Declaration of Independence

This is part of what Jefferson wrote in the Declaration of Independence:

"We hold these truths to be self-evident, that all men are created equal, that they are endowed by their Creator with certain unalienable Rights [rights that cannot be taken away], that among these are Life, Liberty, and the pursuit of Happiness. That to secure these rights, Governments…[get] their just powers from the consent of the governed. That whenever any Form of Government becomes destructive of these ends, it is the Right of the People to alter or to abolish it, and to institute [put into place] new Government…."

Benjamin Franklin (left) and John Adams (center) read the declaration as Thomas Jefferson looks on.

"We, therefore, the Representatives of the united States of America…do…declare, That these United Colonies are, and of Right ought to be Free and Independent States…and that all political connection between them and the State of Great Britain, is and ought to be totally dissolved [ended]."

The War Arrives in Philadelphia

After the Declaration of Independence was signed, Congress had to raise money to fight the American Revolution. It also had to get help from other countries and to set up a new government. Battles continued between British and American armies. During 1776, the British took over New York City and much of New Jersey. Late that year, Washington's army captured Trenton, New Jersey, and at the beginning of 1777, Washington won the Battle of Princeton in New Jersey.

On July 4, 1777, Philadelphia celebrated one year of independence. The city bells rang, and fireworks lit the sky. But in August, a British army under General William Howe landed nearby. Washington's troops could not stop the British. The Continental Congress left the city.

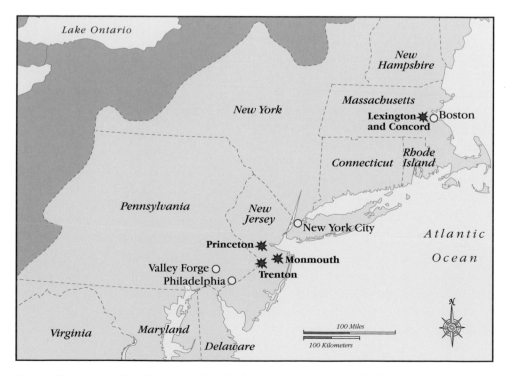

Several important battles were fought in New Jersey, near Philadelphia.

Washington (center, on horseback) and the Marquis de Lafayette (right) talk with troops at Valley Forge.

British troops arrived in Philadelphia on September 26, 1777. George Washington's army moved to Valley Forge, about 20 miles (32 kilometers) northwest of the city, where the soldiers spent a terrible winter without enough food or warm clothing. Meanwhile, the British made life in Philadelphia very different. There was not enough food in the city, and everything cost more.

Then, in June of 1778, the British army left Philadelphia. The State House was so dirty that at first Congress could not meet there. Finally, Congress returned to the city.

Victory at Yorktown

After the British left Philadelphia, American troops attacked them at Monmouth, New Jersey. But in the dark, the British slipped away and escaped into New York City. This was the last big battle in the Northeast. Over the next three years, many battles were fought farther west and in the South. Then, in October 1781, a large British army surrendered to the Americans, who were helped by French troops and a French fleet, at Yorktown, Virginia. The new country, the United States of America, had won the war. The peace treaty officially ending the war was signed by the United States and Great Britain in 1783.

Creating a New Government

While the American Revolution was being fought, the delegates to the Continental Congress created a new government. Their plan, the Articles of Confederation, was approved by all the states in 1781. But after the war, this government had many problems. The states were more powerful than the national government, so they did not follow the laws Congress passed. The states disagreed with each other about trade. They did not send the national government the money it needed.

In 1783, Congress was meeting in Philadelphia when soldiers surrounded the State House because they wanted Pennsylvania to give them the back pay it owed them. This scared Congress, and it moved out of Philadelphia. It finally settled in New York City.

In 1786, a meeting was called to discuss trade between the states, but only five states sent delegates. The delegates decided to hold a convention in Philadelphia the following year to discuss changing the Articles of Confederation.

Arriving in Philadelphia

In May 1787, delegates began arriving. It took many weeks for the 55 delegates, from 12 states, to arrive. Only Rhode Island did not send anyone. These Founding Fathers had worked in their state governments, and many had been in the Continental Congress. Eight had signed the Declaration of Independence. Six had signed the Articles of Confederation. Many had fought in the Revolution.

Meetings and Problems

The delegates met in the State House's Assembly Room from 10:00 A.M. until 3:00 P.M. six days a week for five months. The only holiday they took was the Fourth of July.

They elected George Washington as the convention's president. The delegates decided that the meetings would be secret and that they would

George Washington looks on as a delegate signs the new U.S. Constitution at the end of the convention.

James Madison (1751–1836)

James Madison was born in Virginia in 1751. During the Revolution, he was a member of the Virginia **legislature** for part of the time. He was also a member of the Continental Congress, where he saw the problems of a weak national government. For a year before the Constitutional Convention, he studied books about types of government that Thomas Jefferson had sent him from France. (Madison and Jefferson were close friends.) Madison prepared a plan for what he thought the new United States government should be like. Many of his ideas about the new government were accepted at the Constitutional Convention. He was later given the nickname "Father of the Constitution." Madison also kept notes of everything that happened at the convention, but he did not share them. When he died, almost 50 years later, his notes were published, and Americans learned what really happened at the Constitutional Convention.

When Thomas Jefferson was president, Madison was secretary of state. In 1808 and again in 1812, Madison was elected president of the United States. He was president during the War of 1812 against Great Britain.

not discuss what happened with anyone who was not a delegate. They kept the windows closed so no one could hear what they said, even though it was very hot that summer.

The delegates agreed on some topics, like the need for changes. They did not agree on many topics, including just how strong the new government should be. Because they had so many different ideas, they had to **compromise**. When people who disagree compromise, each side gives up something it wants in order to keep something else it wants even more.

Some delegates were afraid that a very strong government would take too much power from the states. Everyone worked to find a balance between the powers of the new government and the powers of the states. The delegates also tried to make sure that all states, large and small, were treated fairly. They had to think about what the southern states wanted and what the northern states wanted. Slavery was very common in the South. The delegates had to decide whether African-American slaves should be counted as part of the population. They disagreed about whether voters or the state legislatures should pick the members of Congress. There were times when the delegates wanted to leave and go home, and some did.

Benjamin Franklin's Sedan Chair

By 1787, Benjamin Franklin was 81 years old. He was not well and in pain, but he wanted to be part of the Constitutional Convention because he believed it was so important. Every day he came to the meetings carried in a sedan chair. The sedan chair was a box with windows and a chair inside. It was on two long poles and was carried by four strong prisoners from the nearby jail. They brought Franklin right into the Assembly Room and returned every afternoon to get him.

Benjamin Franklin, in his sedan chair, stops to chat on his way to Independence Hall for a meeting of the Constitutional Convention.

In Their Own Words

A Rising Sun

The chair that George Washington used during the Constitutional Convention had a sun painted on its back. At the end of the convention Benjamin Franklin was filled with hope for the new country and said:

> "I have often...looked at that [sun] behind [Washington] without being able to tell whether [it] was rising or setting. But now...I have the happiness to know that it is a rising and not setting sun."

Visitors to Independence Hall can see the chair that Washington used at the Constitutional Convention.

The delegates studied a plan from the Virginia delegates, a plan that was mostly written by James Madison. Not everyone liked it. It had three branches of government: the **executive** branch (headed by the president), the legislative branch (Congress), and the **judicial** branch (courts). Although these branches were separate, the plan had what is known as checks and balances. Each branch had some control over the other two, so that one branch could not become too powerful. Some delegates did not like the legislative branch in this plan, in which Congress had two parts (or houses) and in both of them the larger states had more votes than the smaller states. Then, New Jersey presented a different plan. In its plan, Congress had only one house in which every state had the same number of votes. Many delegates did not agree with this plan, either.

Finally, the delegates compromised. Congress would have two houses: the Senate and the House of Representatives. Every state would have the same number of votes in the Senate, and senators would be chosen by the state legislatures. (This was changed in 1913, so that today the voters in each state elect their senators.) In the House of Representatives, a state with more people would have more representatives. Voters would elect these representatives. Every ten years everybody in the United States would be counted to adjust the number of representatives from each state. This count is called a census. The delegates agreed that three-fifths of the slave population would be counted. This allowed southern states to have a bigger voice than if only free people were counted.

Ratifying the Constitution

Finally, the delegates agreed on what the Constitution would say, and on September 17 it was read to the 41 delegates still at the convention. They listened and made a small change. Then thirty-eight men signed it. One signed the name of a sick delegate, so there are thirty-nine names on the document. However, three delegates refused to sign. The delegates had agreed that each state should hold a special meeting to ratify the Constitution. When nine states ratified it, the new government would start.

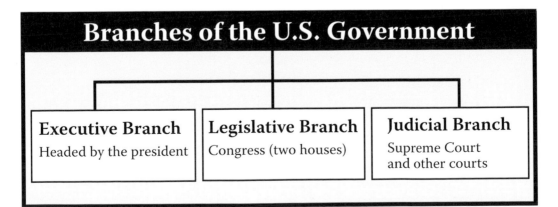

Branches of the U.S. Government

Executive Branch	**Legislative Branch**	**Judicial Branch**
Headed by the president	Congress (two houses)	Supreme Court and other courts

Americans took sides on the Constitution. Those who supported the Constitution were called Federalists. The Federalists thought it was a good plan. Many wanted some changes, but they thought these could be added after the Constitution was ratified. The people against the Constitution were called Anti-Federalists. Anti-Federalists had different reasons for not wanting this Constitution. Some did not like it because they did not want their state to lose power. Others felt it did not protect the rights of individuals. The Federalists and Anti-Federalists wrote newspaper articles and letters, and they gave speeches.

The Pennsylvania convention to ratify the Constitution was held at the State House in November 1787. Most of the delegates were Federalists. Many people came to the Assembly Room to watch the discussion, which lasted about three weeks. On December 12, 1787, the Pennsylvania convention voted to ratify the Constitution. Pennsylvania was the second state to ratify, after Delaware.

Other states soon held their conventions. On June 21, 1788, New Hampshire became the ninth state to ratify the Constitution. The government quickly began work. In February 1789, George Washington was elected president of the new country. In April, Congress began meeting in New York City. Since so many people wanted a bill of rights to protect individuals, it was added on December 15, 1791.

The Bill of Rights

The first ten amendments to the Constitution are called the Bill of Rights. They were added to the Constitution in 1791 to give important protections to individuals. Amendments included in the Bill of Rights guarantee people such things as freedom of speech, freedom to practice any religion they choose, and the right to fair treatment if accused of a crime.

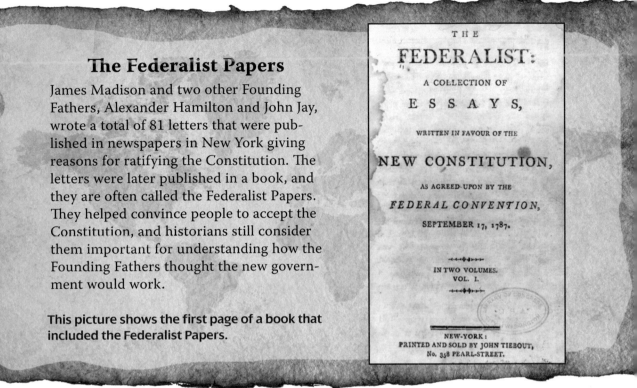

The Federalist Papers

James Madison and two other Founding Fathers, Alexander Hamilton and John Jay, wrote a total of 81 letters that were published in newspapers in New York giving reasons for ratifying the Constitution. The letters were later published in a book, and they are often called the Federalist Papers. They helped convince people to accept the Constitution, and historians still consider them important for understanding how the Founding Fathers thought the new government would work.

This picture shows the first page of a book that included the Federalist Papers.

THE
FEDERALIST:
A COLLECTION OF
E S S A Y S,
WRITTEN IN FAVOUR OF THE
NEW CONSTITUTION,
AS AGREED-UPON BY THE
FEDERAL CONVENTION,
SEPTEMBER 17, 1787.

IN TWO VOLUMES.
VOL. I.

NEW-YORK:
PRINTED AND SOLD BY JOHN TIEBOUT,
No. 358 PEARL-STREET.

Philadelphia, the Capital of the United States

A new capital city was to be built between Maryland and Virginia. Until it was built, Philadelphia was the capital of the United States for ten years beginning in 1790. Congress met in a new courthouse building (its name was changed to Congress Hall). Other government offices were in buildings all over the city. Pennsylvania's state government met in the State House, and the city shared City Hall with the U.S. Supreme Court.

Then, in 1799, the Pennsylvania state government moved to Lancaster (it later moved again, to Harrisburg). In 1800, the United States government moved to its new capital, Washington, D.C. Philadelphia was suddenly much less crowded. Few people talked about the important events that had happened in the State House.

From State House to Independence Hall

After the U.S. and state governments moved out of Philadelphia, the city government used the State House. Side buildings were torn down, and new fire-proof offices were built. The state still owned the building. Later, when the state government decided to sell it, the city bought it and still owns it.

Between 1802 and 1827, artist Charles Willson Peale rented space in the State House. He had a museum that included **portraits** of famous Americans and his many other collections. Many people visited it, but few thought about the great events that had happened in the building

In 1824, Congress invited the Marquis de Lafayette to visit the United States. He had visited the State House during the Revolution and was a popular war hero. Lafayette was greeted with a parade, bands, and speeches at the State House. The mayor called the

Assembly Room the "Hall of Independence" because the Declaration of Independence had been adopted and signed there. From then on, people called this room the Hall of Independence or Independence Hall. Later, people began calling the whole building Independence Hall.

Independence Hall and Slavery

For many years, the U.S. Marshals Service and a federal court used the second floor of the State House. U.S. marshals make sure court decisions are followed. The Fugitive Slave Act of 1850 said that escaped slaves had to be returned to their owners. The marshals arrested African Americans

This picture shows the inside of Independence Hall as it looked in the 1850s.

Peale's Museum

Charles Willson Peale was a painter, but he was also interested in many other things. He had hundreds of animals, live and stuffed, including bears, eagles, and snakes. In 1801, he helped excavate (dig up) the first skeleton of a mastodon found in the United States. Mastodons, which no longer exist, were elephant-like animals with shaggy hair and huge tusks. This one was 11 feet (3.4 meters) high and 15 feet (4.6 meters) long, and it had tusks that were 11 feet (3.4 meters) long. Peale brought the bones back to Philadelphia and displayed the skeleton in his museum. For many years, Peale's live animals ate grass in the State House Yard. By 1818, the museum also had 180 portraits painted by Peale, his son, or his brother.

thought to have escaped from slavery in the South and to have come to the North, where slavery had been abolished. If the court decided that these people were guilty of escaping, they were returned to their owners. Many people were unhappy that this was happening in the building that was a symbol of freedom. The strong disagreements between the North and the South over slavery led to the Civil War (1861–1865). After the North won the war, slavery was abolished throughout the United States in 1865.

Late in the nineteenth century, Philadelphia's city government moved into a new building. When this happened, in 1895, the State House for the first time did not have any government offices in it.

A Place for Celebrations and Demonstrations

The State House Yard had always been a place where people got together to celebrate and to express their opinions. It was renamed Independence Square in 1825.

July 4, 1826, was the 50th anniversary of the United States. It was also the day Thomas Jefferson and John Adams died. In their honor, on July 24, bells rang, but with a muffled sound. There was a slow parade to

Independence Square. People gathered in the Hall of Independence, where they heard speeches about these two Founding Fathers.

In later years, presidents visited Independence Hall and gave speeches, as Andrew Jackson did in 1833. In 1861, Abraham Lincoln stopped at Independence Hall on his way to Washington, D.C., to be sworn in as president. He spoke to a large crowd in Independence Square. Then, in 1865, he was shot and killed. His body was taken back to Illinois to be buried, but there were stops at many places along the way.

"The Boys in Blue,"
RETURNING THE STATE FLAGS TO THE GOVERNOR OF PENNSYLVANIA,
Independence Square, Philadelphia, July 4th, 1866.

The steeple of Independence Hall was covered in flags for a huge celebration to honor Civil War soldiers on July 4, 1866.

In Independence Hall, many people walked by his coffin to honor him.

On the Fourth of July in 1866, Philadelphia had a huge celebration to honor the men who had fought in the Civil War. There were flags all over Independence Hall and a parade to Independence Square. That day the governor of Pennsylvania reminded people that this building was "the birthplace of American liberty."

In 1876, a Centennial Exhibition was held in Philadelphia for the country's 100th birthday. It was held 5 miles (8 kilometers) from Inde-

There were celebrations at Independence Hall in 1876 for the 100th anniversary of the Declaration of Independence.

pendence Square, but pictures of Independence Hall and the Liberty Bell appeared in newspapers and magazines and on many souvenirs. Two big events took place at Independence Hall that year. On 1875's rainy New Year's Eve, thousands of people gathered near Independence Hall. At midnight, when it became 1876, bells rang for 30 minutes while people cheered and a huge flag was unrolled. Then, on the Fourth of July, another huge celebration was held in Independence Square. It included a parade with thousands of people and a speech by Vice President Henry Wilson.

Other demonstrations in Independence Square were not so joyful. Sometimes they ended with violence and fights. Workers in the 1830s demonstrated for better working conditions. They did not want to work ten hours a day. Before the Civil War, people such as the **abolitionist** Frederick Douglass spoke against slavery.

There were demonstrations in the twentieth century as well. In the 1960s, during the civil rights movement, people demonstrated in favor of equal rights for all Americans, especially African Americans. In the late 1960s and early 1970s, people demonstrated because they did not like the Vietnam War, in which the United States was fighting at that time.

In Their Own Words

Women's Right to Vote

Women did not have the right to vote in 1876. **Suffragists** were women who were working to get the vote. When Vice President Henry Wilson finished speaking on July 4, 1876, five suffragists handed him a paper about giving women the vote. Then they left, and on a nearby street, they read it aloud. One part said:

"We cannot forget, even in this glad hour, that while all men of every race… have…the full rights of citizenship under our hospitable flag, all women still suffer…disfranchisement [not being allowed to vote]."

A Place to Honor the Past

The Assembly Room, or Hall of Independence, was redecorated several times. In 1876, when it was redone, it looked much fancier than it had been in 1776. For a while the National Museum was in the building. This museum displayed things that people had saved from the time of the American Revolution.

Over the years, the building needed many repairs. In 1896, the two side office buildings that the city had built in 1812 were torn down, and new ones were built. These new ones looked more like the original buildings. In 1898, the Philadelphia chapter of American Institute of Architects (AIA) created a committee to help the city restore the building. The AIA committee used information from the past to make decisions on how to fix the building, so that it would look very much as it did in the 1700s.

During these years, Philadelphia was changing, too. Large warehouses and tall office buildings were built near Independence Hall. Tourists still came to see Independence Hall, but most had trouble imagining what the city looked like during the Revolution. The modern city seemed to be hiding the past.

The Liberty Bell

No one is sure exactly when the Liberty Bell began to crack, but it last rang on George Washington's birthday (February 22) in 1846, when the crack began getting larger.

In 1847, author George Lippard wrote a story about the bell. He told about a boy who listened at the door of the Continental Congress. He raced to tell his grandfather to ring the bell when Congress decided on

This photograph shows Independence Hall around 1900.

The Justice Bell

Suffragists had a bell just like the Liberty Bell. They called it the Justice Bell. Its clapper was chained to the side, so that it could not ring. This symbolized that women did not have justice because they did not have the right to vote. When women got the vote in 1920, suffragists brought the Justice Bell to Independence Hall. They untied the clapper and rang the bell. Today the Justice Bell is at Valley Forge National Park.

Suffragists with the Justice Bell as they worked to gain for women the right to vote.

independence. It did not happen, though. The wood in the bell tower was very rotten in 1776. It is believed that it would have been too dangerous to ring that bell. But in the 1800s, people believed this legend, and it made the bell into a popular symbol of American freedom.

From 1885 until 1915, the Liberty Bell traveled by train to many parts of the United States. It stopped in small towns and large cities, including New Orleans, Chicago, and Charleston, South Carolina. It went to Bunker Hill in Boston, where one of the first battles of the American Revolution had been fought, and thousands of people came to see it. They wanted to see this symbol and were curious about its crack. Then, just before it went to San Francisco in 1915, another crack was discovered. For this last trip, the bell had its own train.

Visiting Independence Hall Today

Over the years, many people worked to protect Independence Hall. Then, beginning in the early 1940s, some people wanted to create a historic area that would also include many of the historic buildings near it.

In 1943, Independence Hall became a national historic site, and the National Park Service took over its care. The city still owns it, though. In 1948, President Harry Truman created Independence National Historical Park, which includes Independence Hall and several other buildings. A few years earlier, the state was planning Independence Mall State Park. Many buildings in the area near Independence Hall were torn down to create this park. Later, the state had the National Park Service manage the park. It eventually became part of Independence National Historical Park.

Besides Independence Hall, there are many historic buildings in the area. Some are run by the National Park Service. Others, like

Symbols on Money and Stamps

The United States government uses symbols, including Independence Hall and the Liberty Bell, on its money and stamps. Independence Hall is on the back of the $100 bill and the 1975 and 1976 Kennedy half-dollar. On the back of the $2 bill is a painting by John Trumbull called "The Signing of the Declaration of Independence." In 1926, for the 150th anniversary of the Declaration, a 2-cent stamp with a picture of the Liberty Bell on it was issued, and so was a special half-dollar coin with Independence Hall on it. Independence Hall was put on a 10-cent stamp in 1956. The Liberty Bell was on a 13-cent stamp in 1975 for the 200th birthday of the United States.

Carpenters' Hall, are private buildings. A few buildings, like the Liberty Bell Center and the National Constitution Center, are new (both opened in 2003). Most tell a story about the Declaration of Independence, the Constitution, the federal government, or life in Philadelphia around 1790.

Visiting the Historic Area

In the historic part of Philadelphia, visitors can look into the life of people in the past and explore how ideas from the past affect life today. Most people visiting the area start at the Independence Visitor Center to decide where to visit. They get tickets for tours because Independence Hall and several other buildings can be seen only on a tour. Places to visit include the following:

Independence Hall is where the Founding Fathers adopted the Declaration of Independence and the Constitution. Visitors can see the Assembly Room as it was at that time. They can also visit the West Wing building, which holds *The Great Essentials* exhibit. It has copies of the Declaration of Independence and the Constitution.

The Liberty Bell Center is a new building. Exhibits show how the bell has been used as a symbol for freedom. The bell is in a glass room, and Independence Hall can be seen through the window behind it.

Independence Hall and many other historic sites are within a few blocks of one another.

Carpenters' Hall was designed and built in the 1770s by the Carpenters' Company, which still owns the building. The First Continental Congress met there in 1774.

Franklin Court is where Benjamin Franklin's house used to be. Steel beams outline where it was. An underground museum has paintings, objects, and inventions associated with Franklin. There is also a printing office, and visitors can see how Franklin printed newspapers and books.

The Betsy Ross House is where Betsy Ross lived and is said to have made the new country's first flag. Today, visitors going through the house can get an idea of what home life was like in colonial times.

The Todd House is where Dolley Todd lived with her husband, John. He died of yellow fever in 1793. Less than a year later she married James Madison, who was in Congress at the time. When he was elected the fourth president, she became the First Lady and was known for her parties. She is famous for saving George Washington's portrait from the White House just before the building was burned by British troops during the War of 1812.

Betsy Ross and the First Flag

The story of Betsy Ross and the first American flag was kept alive by the Ross family. They told it to their children, who told it to their children. Finally, in 1870, the family told the story to the world. They said that during the Second Continental Congress, a committee including George Washington came to see Betsy Ross. The men showed her a design for a flag and asked her to make it. She suggested they change the star from one with six points to one with five points. Then she promised to try to make what they wanted. There are no written records to prove she made this first flag. But whether her story is true or not, it has become an American legend.

In this painting, Betsy Ross (right) explains how she made her flag. George Washington is seated on the left.

The Liberty Medal

The National Constitution Center awards the Liberty Medal every year to a person or organization that is working for freedom and to improve people's lives. U.S. Supreme Court Justice Sandra Day O'Connor won it for supporting justice and fairness in the United States. Nelson Mandela and F. W. de Klerk shared the medal for their work to improve the rights of black people in South Africa. The organization Doctors Without Borders got the medal for its work to provide medical and other help to suffering people around the world.

Congress Hall is next to Independence Hall. The United States Congress met there from 1790 to 1800. George Washington was inaugurated there for his second term as president. Later, the building was used as a courthouse. Today, it looks as it might have in 1790.

The First Bank of the United States is the oldest bank building in the United States. It was built between 1795 and 1797 and restored for the 200th birthday of the United States.

The Second Bank of the United States building has a large collection of portraits of people important during and after the American Revolution.

Many of these portraits were painted by the artist Charles Willson Peale.

At the National Constitution Center, which opened in 2003, visitors can learn about the document that for more than 200 years has been the basis for the kind of government the United States has.

The Assembly Room is set up today to look as it did when the Continental Congress met there to adopt the Declaration of Independence.

Old City Hall was used by the U.S. Supreme Court from 1791 to 1800, as well as being used by the city government. The building now has exhibits about the U.S. Supreme Court and life in Philadelphia in the 1790s.

The National Constitution Center is a new museum. It has interactive exhibits about the U.S. Constitution. Visitors can take part in many activities, such as choosing their favorite president. One room has life-sized statues of the 39 men whose names are on the Constitution and the three delegates who refused to sign it.

City with a Historic Heart

Today, Philadelphia is a city that has a historic heart, or area, that tells the story of the birth of the United States. This area, with Independence Hall at its center, reminds people of the ideas of freedom and independence that were so important to the Founding Fathers and that have been important throughout the history of the United States.

Timeline ★ ★ ★ ★ ★ ★ ★ ★ ★

★ **1732–1742**   The Pennsylvania State House is built.

★ **1753**   A new bell cracks when rung for the first time, is remade twice, and is then hung in the State House steeple.

★ **1774**   The First Continental Congress meets at Carpenters' Hall.

★ **1775**   The Second Continental Congress begins meeting in the State House's Assembly Room.

★ **1776**   **July 4:** Congress approves the Declaration of Independence at the State House. **July 8:** The Declaration of Independence is read in the State House Yard.

★ **1777**   **September 26:** British troops capture Philadelphia.

★ **1778**   **June 18:** British troops leave Philadelphia.

★ **1781**   The American victory at the Battle of Yorktown ensures American independence.

★ **1783**   The treaty officially ending the American Revolution is signed.

★ **1787**   **May:** The Constitutional Convention begins meeting at the State House. **September 17:** The U.S. Constitution is signed in the Assembly Room.

★ **1790**   The U.S. government moves to Philadelphia.

★ **1800**   The U.S. government leaves Philadelphia for Washington, D.C.

★ **1824**   The Assembly Room becomes known as the Hall of Independence. Eventually, the building becomes known as Independence Hall.

★ **1825**   The State House Yard is renamed Independence Square.

★ **1830s**   People who want to end slavery call the State House bell the "Liberty Bell."

★ **1846**   A crack is found in the Liberty Bell after it rings for George Washington's birthday.

★ **1943**   Independence Hall becomes a national historic site.

★ **2003**   The Liberty Bell is moved to the new Liberty Bell Center.

abolitionist: Someone who wanted to end slavery.

adopted: Officially accepted; approved.

assembly: A group of people who meet together for a purpose, such as to write laws.

capital: A city where a government is located.

clapper: The part inside a bell that hits the outer part and makes it ring.

colonies: Places where people have settled but remain under another country's government.

committee: A group that works together for a certain purpose.

compromise: An agreement or a decision in which each side gives up something it wants to get something it wants even more.

constitution: A written plan of government.

convention: A meeting organized for a specific purpose, such as to make an important decision.

delegate: A person chosen to represent others.

demonstration: A large gathering where people show their feelings on a specific topic.

executive: A person who manages something; in government, it is the branch that carries out laws.

independence: Freedom from the control of someone or something else.

judicial: Having to do with courts and judges.

legislature: A group of people who meet to write laws. A legislative branch of government includes the legislature.

plantation: A large farm on which crops are grown to be sold.

portrait: A painting of a person (or sometimes of a group of people).

Quakers: A religious group that developed in England in the 1600s and that had some beliefs that were different from those of the official English church.

representative: Someone who acts for someone else or for a group of people; people elect representatives to act for them in government.

representation: Acting in the place of someone else or of a group of people with their consent.

steeple: A tower on top of a building that comes to a point at the top and often holds a bell.

suffragists: People who worked for women's right to vote.

symbol: Something that stands for something else, often an idea or a place.

To Learn More ★ ★ ★ ★ ★ ★ ★

Read these books

Fink, Sam. *The Declaration of Independence*. New York: Scholastic, 2002.

Gunderson, Jessica. *The Second Continental Congress*. Mankato, Minn.: Capstone Press, 2008.

Jango-Cohen, Judith. *The Liberty Bell*. Minneapolis, Minn.: Lerner Publishing, 2003.

Magaziner, Henry Jonas. *Our Liberty Bell*. New York: Holiday House, 2007.

Marcovitz, Hal. *Independence Hall*. Broomall, Penn.: Mason Crest Publishers, 2002.

Miller, Brandon Marie. *Declaring Independence: Life During the American Revolution*. Minneapolis, Minn.: Lerner Publishing, 2005.

Schaefer, Ted, and Lola M. Schaefer. *Independence Hall*. Chicago: Heinemann Library, 2005.

Swain, Gwenyth. *Declaring Freedom: A Look at the Declaration of Independence, the Bill of Rights, and the Constitution*. Minneapolis, Minn.: Lerner Publishing, 2003.

Look up these Web sites

Independence National Historical Park Official Website
http://www.nps.gov/inde/index.htm

Liberty Bell Virtual Museum
http://www.libertybellmuseum.com

Library of Congress Exhibit: Declaring Independence: Drafting the Documents
http://www.loc.gov/exhibits/declara/declara1.html

National Constitution Center Official Website
http://www.constitutioncenter.org

Timeline of the American Revolution
http://www.nps.gov/revwar/about_the_revolution/timeline_of_events.html

Key Internet search terms

American Revolution, Constitutional Convention, Declaration of Independence, Independence Hall, Thomas Jefferson, U.S. Constitution

The abbreviation *ill.* stands for illustration, and *ills.* stands for illustrations. Page references to illustrations and maps are in *italic* type.

Index ★ ★ ★ ★ ★ ★ ★ ★ ★ ★ ★

About the Author

Hilarie Staton has written for students and teachers for more than twenty-five years. She enjoys researching and writing about history, especially using original documents. She lives in the Hudson Valley, an area where she finds many American history stories to tell. Other books about history she has written include *The Progressive Party: The Success of a Failed Party*.